Dolley Madison

History Maker Bios

Jean L. S. Patrick

LERNER PUBLICATIONS COMPANY • MINNEAPOLIS

For my daughter, Catherine—faithful research assistant, carsick navigator, wonderful friend

The author would like to thank those who provided assistance, including Holly C. Shulman, University of Virginia; Allison Enos, Lee Langston-Harrison, and Lynne Lewis of James Madison's Montpelier; and the generous people from the James Madison Museum, the Orange County Historical Society, The Papers of James Madison, the University of Virginia Library-Special Collections, the Virginia Historical Society, and the Virginia Transportation Research Council.

Illustrations by Tim Parlin.

Text copyright © 2002 by Jean L. S. Patrick
Illustrations copyright © 2002 by Lerner Publications Company

Lerner Publications Company
A division of Lerner Publishing Group
241 First Avenue North
Minneapolis, MN 55401 U.S.A.

Website address: www.lernerbooks.com

Library of Congress Cataloging-in-Publication Data

Patrick, Jean L. S.
    Dolley Madison / by Jean L. S. Patrick.
        p.   cm. — (History maker bios)
    Includes bibliographical references and index.
    Summary: A biography of the popular and dynamic wife of our fourth president, James Madison.
        ISBN: 0–8225–0194–5 (lib. bdg. : alk. paper)
    1. Madison, Dolley, 1768–1849—Juvenile literature. 2. Presidents' spouses—United States—Biography—Juvenile literature. [1. Madison, Dolley, 1768–1849. 2. First ladies. 3. Women—Biography.] I. Title. II. Series.
    E342.1.M2 P38 2002
    973.5'1'092—dc21   2001003277

Manufactured in the United States of America
1 2 3 4 5 6 – JR – 07 06 05 04 03 02

TABLE OF CONTENTS

INTRODUCTION

Does the name Dolley Madison make you think of Easter eggs? According to legend, Dolley decorated eggs and invited children to play with them on the lawn of the Capitol in Washington. But there's more to Dolley than Easter eggs.

Dolley Madison was the wife of James Madison, the fourth president of the United States. She opened the President's House to the people and made everyone feel welcome. Dolley also inspired people with her courage. When the British attacked Washington during the War of 1812, Dolley rescued a national treasure. Dolley Madison loved her country and its people.

This is her story.

1 GOOD-BYE, VIRGINIA

Thirteen-year-old Dolley Payne gazed across the green fields of her family's Virginia plantation. All looked calm. But the year was 1781. The United States was fighting for independence from Great Britain. At last report, British soldiers were burning buildings in nearby villages. Would her father protect their home?

Dolley didn't know. She and her family were Quakers. They refused to fight, not even in war.

Dolley had always been a Quaker. She was born on May 20, 1768, in Guilford County, North Carolina. Now she lived at the Coles Hill Plantation in Hanover County, Virginia.

Fortunately, the British never attacked her home. Instead they surrendered to General George Washington in October 1781. Less than two years later, the war was over. Dolley's country was free.

A woman works as she attends a Quaker meeting.

President Washington's second inauguration was held in Philadelphia in 1793.

Near the end of the war, Dolley's parents decided to free their slaves. This was very brave. Without slaves to work in the fields, the plantation could not survive. What would Dolley's family do?

Fifteen-year-old Dolley helped load the wagons. She and her family were moving to Philadelphia, the largest city in the United States.

What a change! People were everywhere. Fancy carriages rolled down narrow streets. Women wore earrings and elegant dresses.

Most Quakers didn't wear elegant clothes, so Dolley's dresses were plain and gray. But she still had fun. With other young Quakers, Dolley went sailing, had picnics, and worshipped at the Pine Street Meeting House.

Life was harder for Dolley's father. The starch business he had opened wasn't doing well. When he couldn't pay his bills, the Quakers asked him to leave their group. Later, Dolley's mother opened a boardinghouse to support their family.

DOLLEY'S SECRET

During Dolley's lifetime, Quakers wore simple clothing. As a child, Dolley wore long gray dresses with long gray sleeves. No decorations were allowed. But Dolley may have disobeyed. Some people say that her grandmother (who was not a Quaker) gave her jewelry that Dolley wore hidden underneath her dress.

Dolley and John Todd lived in this large brick house on the corner of Fourth and Walnut Streets.

In January of 1790, Dolley married a Quaker lawyer named John Todd. Their son Payne was born two years later. In 1793, baby William arrived.

Then, terror struck Philadelphia.

Yellow fever! Hundreds of people died each week. Dolley held her sons tightly as she hurried away from the city. But sadness followed. On October 24, 1793, her husband died. Baby William died, too. Dolley and Payne survived.

By springtime, the threat of yellow fever had passed. Dolley was still in mourning. But she was so beautiful that men would stand on street corners just to watch her walk by.

Her best friend, Eliza Collins, gasped, "Really, Dolley, thou must hide thy face—there are so many staring at thee!"

Dolley was sure Eliza was teasing. But one of the men asked to meet her. His name was James Madison.

James Madison was known as the Great Little Madison. Both James and Dolley were about five feet six inches tall.

People were charmed by Dolley's blue eyes, black curls, and warm personality.

Dolley was surprised. James Madison had helped write the Constitution. Now he was a congressman and helped make decisions for the country. He even gave advice to President George Washington.

Their romance moved quickly. Within a few months, James asked her to marry him. But Dolley needed time to think.

Dolley was twenty-six years old and loved to be with people. James was forty-three years old and rather shy. She was a Quaker. He was not. If she married him, she could no longer be a Quaker.

Finally, Dolley agreed. On September 15, 1794, she and James were married.

Dolley's simple life changed. As the wife of a congressman, she attended balls and wore colorful dresses. Dolley was happy. She was surrounded by people.

When James left Congress in 1797, the Madisons moved to Montpelier. This was the home of James's parents in Orange County, Virginia. James managed the five-thousand-acre plantation while Dolley cared for her family.

But the Madisons did not stay at Montpelier. Four years later, they moved again.

2 WELCOME TO WASHINGTON

Dolley, James, nine-year-old Payne, and Dolley's sister Anna arrived in the city of Washington on May 1, 1801. The land was swampy. Tree stumps stood in the middle of the road. The city's buildings were half-finished.

Dolley was excited. Washington wasn't just a new city. It was the new capital of the United States. President Thomas Jefferson had chosen James to help him as secretary of state.

James was not the only one with a new job. On May 27, Dolley received a note from President Jefferson. Would she or her sister Anna like to dine with him and his guests? He needed someone to entertain the women.

Dolley agreed. President Jefferson's wife had died years ago, and he needed help. After all, he even greeted guests in his slippers!

Dolley was very close to her sister Anna, who was eleven years younger than she was. Dolley called Anna her sister-child.

WESTERN ADVENTURE

In 1803, Dolley gave a farewell party at her home for Meriwether Lewis and William Clark. They were going to explore the lands west of the Mississippi River. When Lewis and Clark returned, they told Dolley about their adventures and gave her the silver cooking utensils they had used on their trip.

For the next eight years, Dolley served as Jefferson's hostess. She welcomed important leaders to the President's House. She never forgot a name or a face.

Dolley also held parties in her own home. Soon she had friends all over Washington. Yet she watched her own family grow smaller. In 1804, her sister Anna married and moved to Maine. The next year, thirteen-year-old Payne left for boarding school in Baltimore, Maryland.

Meanwhile, the British were causing problems. They were capturing American ships and kidnapping the sailors.

Would there be another war against Great Britain? Not yet.

On March 4, 1809, James Madison became the fourth president of the United States. As the president's wife, Dolley had plans. She wanted to reach out to the people of Washington. She wanted the President's House to be a place where many people could meet peacefully, even if they had different opinions.

When James Madison was president, most people called his Washington home the President's House, not the White House.

So Dolley began to remodel. An architect named Benjamin Latrobe helped.

They decorated the sitting room in yellow, Dolley's favorite color. In the drawing room, they hung 150 yards of red velvet curtains. Next, they enlarged the dining room. At the head of the room, they hung a huge portrait of George Washington. It was eight feet tall.

After the work was done, Dolley opened the President's House to everyone. Each Wednesday night, people would gather to drink punch, eat cake, and talk to the president.

Dolley wore the latest in French fashion. Her colorful dresses had high waists, low necks, and short sleeves. On her head, she wore turbans, often topped with tall feathers. She looked like a queen.

But Dolley didn't want to act like a queen. She walked through the crowded rooms talking warmly with her guests, especially those who were alone.

Dolley loved to wear elegant clothing.

With grace, Dolley encouraged people to be peaceful. But she knew that they often disagreed.

Many congressmen from the northern states did not want war with the British. They didn't even want James Madison to be president. But many congressmen from the South and West wanted to fight. They believed that the United States should be respected as a free country.

"I believe there will be War," predicted Dolley in a letter to her sister Anna in December of 1811. Dolley was right. On June 18, 1812, President Madison declared war on Britain.

Americans capture the British ship FROLIC in the fall of 1812.

The next May, British soldiers burned two-thirds of the homes in Havre de Grace, Maryland. Would Washington be next? Dolley still thought of herself as a peaceful Quaker. But if attacked, she was ready to fight.

In the summer of 1814, British ships began to land at Benedict, Maryland. They were just fifty miles away! James warned his leaders of an attack.

But the secretary of war, General John Armstrong, would not protect the city of Washington from the British. "They certainly will not come here," he said.

General Armstrong was wrong.

3 ATTACK!

In August 1814, four thousand British soldiers marched north to Bladensburg. American soldiers prepared to stop them. The people of Washington grew restless. Bladensburg was just seven miles away!

Families fled. The soldiers guarding the President's House vanished. James rode away to check the troops. Dolley stayed in Washington. She had promised James she would wait until he returned.

On Tuesday, August 23, Dolley received a note from James. Be ready to leave the city at a moment's warning, he wrote. The enemy seems stronger than first reported. If they reach the city, they will likely destroy it.

Dolley filled trunks with important government papers and loaded them into a carriage. There would be no room for her own belongings.

Although Dolley couldn't rescue her elegant gowns, she later replaced them.

Not all legends about Dolley are true. This painting shows her saving the Declaration of Independence. But it had already been moved to a place of safety.

Early on the morning of August 24, Dolley peered through her spyglass. Where was her husband? Twice, the mayor urged her to leave Washington. Twice, she refused.

By noon, the temperature reached ninety-eight degrees. An hour later, a cannon boomed. The battle against the British had begun.

Dolley hurried. She packed a second carriage with books, a clock, and the red velvet curtains. Still, she would not leave.

Instead, she calmly arranged for dinner. She hoped that James and his military officers would join her.

Outside, Dolley heard hoofbeats. "Clear out!" yelled James Smith, who had accompanied her husband to battle. "General Armstrong has ordered a retreat!"

Two men, Jacob Barker and Robert DePeyster, charged through the door, offering to help. Dolley knew that she must leave her home. Yet she pointed to George Washington's portrait.

This is the famous portrait of George Washington, painted by Gilbert Stuart, that hung in the President's House.

"Save that picture!" she ordered. "If not possible, destroy it. Under no circumstances allow it to fall into the hands of the British!"

Dolley was firm. The picture was more than a portrait. George Washington was more than a man. He was a symbol of her country and its freedom.

Two servants broke the heavy frame with an axe. Jacob Barker and Robert DePeyster removed the canvas, then rushed it to safety.

Finally, Dolley fled.

Like Dolley, this soldier's wife fought to protect her home during the War of 1812.

British soldiers set fire to the city of Washington.

Later that evening, Dolley learned that James was safe. Relieved, she took shelter at the Virginia home of her friend Matilda Love.

From an open window, Dolley looked back to the city, just ten miles away. Flames flared high on the horizon. Smoke stung her eyes.

Dolley wept. The British were burning Washington. Would her country lose its independence?

Four days later, Dolley returned to the city in a rented carriage. The people cheered.

But Dolley mourned. Dead horses lay in the grass. The roof of the Capitol lay smoldering in its cellar. Her own home had been torched. Nothing remained but its cracked and blackened shell.

Dolley could barely speak. If only she had ten thousand men to sink the enemy into a bottomless pit!

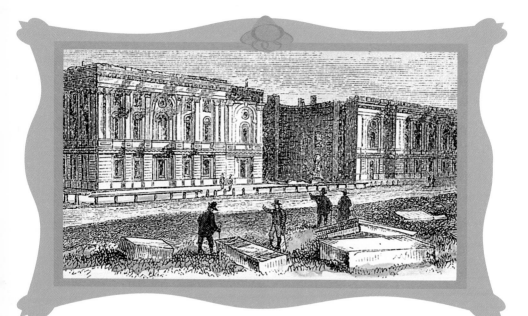

The ruins of the Capitol building. The British fired rockets through the roof.

FLYING CANNONS

On the night the British burned Washington, an explosion killed one hundred of their soldiers. The next day, mighty winds tossed British cannons into the air as heavy rains put out fires in the city. Meanwhile, the British feared that the Americans might regroup and attack. Silently, they left Washington at nightfall.

On September 8, Dolley and James moved into the Octagon House, an elegant home in Washington that stood undamaged. The city began to rebuild.

Although the war continued, Dolley resumed her Wednesday night gatherings. In the brightly painted rooms of the Octagon House, she encouraged people to remain united and strong.

On February 17, 1815, James signed a peace treaty. The war with Britain was over.

"Peace!" cried Dolley's cousin Sally. "Peace!"

Dolley beamed. Congressmen packed the rooms of the Octagon. Instead of disagreeing, they rejoiced together.

A month later, Dolley and James moved a few blocks away to a house called Seven Buildings. Dolley filled their sunny home with secondhand furniture and happy guests.

In March 1817, James's presidency was over. It was time to go home to Montpelier.

4 MONTPELIER

T he road climbed. The carriage swayed. Beyond the red buds of the maple trees, Dolley could see the Blue Ridge Mountains. When they reached Montpelier, she smiled. As James said, they were just a "squirrel's leap" from heaven.

Although Montpelier was nearly one hundred miles from Washington, they had plenty of company.

A portico with four elegant columns frames the entry to Montpelier.

During the summer, Anna and her children stayed and played. Important leaders also visited, asking James for advice about the country's future. Sometimes, Thomas Jefferson came from nearby Monticello, just to talk about farming. Dolley welcomed them all.

In 1828, a friend and her daughter visited from Washington. Dolley grabbed the girl's hand and led her to the front portico.

"Come, let us run a race," she said. "Madison and I often run races here, when the weather does not allow us to walk."

Dolley felt young. She was sixty years old.

Fewer people visited during the winter. This gave Dolley more time to help James with his papers. Over forty years ago, James had taken detailed notes while the Constitution was being written. Now he wanted to prepare these notes for publication.

A group of men, including James Madison, had gathered in 1787 to write the Constitution.

Together, they worked for five hours each day. They read. They copied. They stacked the new sheets in order. The first volume was six hundred pages!

Dolley's eyes hurt. Yet she continued to work. The papers were important to James and to the nation. They were also important to her. James wanted the sale of his papers to provide her with money after he died.

Dolley knew that her life seemed perfect. She had a mountain home, streams of friends, and a husband who loved her.

SLAVERY: A DIFFICULT QUESTION

James Madison didn't know what to do about slavery. He believed slavery was evil, yet he owned more than one hundred slaves at Montpelier. He believed slavery should end, but he didn't think that freed slaves could live in the United States. James despaired, but found no answers.

Dolley's son Payne Todd. Dolley and James spent more than forty thousand dollars on Payne's debts and expenses.

But her heart ached. Her son Payne was nearly forty years old, yet he had no wife, no job, and no money. He also gambled and drank. No matter how much money she and James sent, Payne always needed more. If only he would visit her, just so she could tell him how much she loved him.

Other sadness entered Dolley's life. In 1831, her sister Anna became very sick. But Dolley could not visit her. James was weak with rheumatism. She could not leave him.

During the last five years of James's life, Dolley didn't leave him for more than a half an hour at a time.

Dolley picked up her pen and described her husband to Anna's daughter. "His fingers and hands are still so swollen and sore as to be nearly useless, but I lend him mine."

Four years later, James could not even rise from his bed. A gray-and-white cap covered his head as he leaned against his pillow. But his mind was sharp.

Dolley continued to care for James. She read to him, worked on his papers, and joined him in a project that would honor George Washington with a monument.

Just after breakfast on June 28, 1836, James died. He was eighty-five years old.

Dolley cried. She missed him. Yet he had given her a responsibility. She must place his writings before the country and world.

5 RETURN TO WASHINGTON

The next spring, Congress bought the first three volumes of James's writings. This was good news. But Dolley dreaded spending another lonely winter at Montpelier.

Dolley wondered. Perhaps she could move back to Washington. After all, she owned a two-story house, just a block away from the President's House. It even had plum trees.

In the fall of 1837, Dolley received a grand welcome back to Washington. People invited her to parties. She raised money for an orphanage and attended sessions of Congress. She even dined at the rebuilt President's House, which was now called the White House.

At her home, friends visited every day. New Year's Day and Independence Day were busiest. People greeted the president, then walked to Dolley's house. Dolley sat upon a red ottoman, wearing a black dress, a white turban, and a set of fake black curls. She welcomed everyone.

Washington in about 1830, with the newly rebuilt Capitol in the distance

But Dolley hid a secret. She had no money of her own. The funds from Congress were gone. The Montpelier plantation was not making a profit. For years, she had borrowed money from banks and friends.

Dolley was seventy-six years old. What would she do?

On August 12, 1844, she sold Montpelier. Her hand trembled as she wrote to the new owner, "No one I think, can appreciate my feeling of grief and dismay."

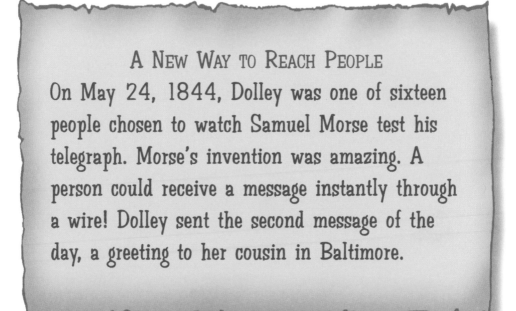

A NEW WAY TO REACH PEOPLE

On May 24, 1844, Dolley was one of sixteen people chosen to watch Samuel Morse test his telegraph. Morse's invention was amazing. A person could receive a message instantly through a wire! Dolley sent the second message of the day, a greeting to her cousin in Baltimore.

But the new owner did not make payments to Dolley. Later that year, Congress refused to buy the rest of the James's writings.

Dolley didn't complain. Wearing her old black dress, she attended receptions at the White House. When guests came to her home, she gave them pieces of her French china as gifts.

On May 20, 1848, Dolley celebrated her eightieth birthday. Her grandnephew ran to her door with a message. Congress had agreed to buy her husband's remaining writings.

The Washington Monument, shown here in about 1855, took more than thirty-five years to complete.

The money would not cover her debts. But Dolley was relieved. James's writings would be preserved for the future.

On Independence Day, Dolley celebrated again. Twenty thousand people gathered to watch the laying of the cornerstone of the Washington Monument.

Years ago, Dolley and James had planned for this monument. Even then, they understood its grand purpose. The monument would honor George Washington and be a symbol of patriotism.

A year later, on July 12, 1849, Dolley Madison died. At her funeral, President Zachary Taylor honored her with a new title. "She will never be forgotten," he said, "because she was truly our First Lady for a half-century."

Dolley's funeral procession was one of the largest in Washington's history. It included the president, all the members of Congress, the officers of the army and navy, her friends, and the citizens of Washington.

Dolley would have been pleased. Everyone was welcome.

TIMELINE

In the year . . .

DOLLEY PAYNE
WAS BORN ON
MAY 20, 1768.

1783 Dolley's family moved to Philadelphia from Virginia.
the Revolutionary War ended.

Age 15

1790 she married John Todd, Jr.

1792 her son John Payne Todd was born.

1793 her son William Temple Todd was born.
her husband and son William died of yellow fever.

1794 she married James Madison on September 15.

Age 26

1801 James became secretary of state and they moved to Washington.

1809 James became president.
she remodeled the President's House.

Age 40

1812 the United States declared war on Britain on June 18.

1814 she saved a portrait of George Washington before the British burned Washington on August 24.

Age 46

1815 James signed a peace treaty to end the War of 1812.

1817 she and James returned to Montpelier.

1836 James died on June 28.

Age 68

1837 Congress bought the first three volumes of James's papers.
she returned to Washington.

1844 she sold Montpelier.

1848 Congress bought the remainder of James's papers.

1849 she died on July 12.

Age 81

DOLLEY'S GINGERBREAD

When people visited the President's House, Dolley Madison often served refreshments. This is a modern version of one of Dolley's favorite recipes. (Her recipe used beef drippings instead of melted butter!)

3 cups flour
1 tablespoon ginger
1 tablespoon cinnamon
½ cup melted butter
1 cup molasses

1 cup hot water
1 teaspoon baking soda dissolved in 1 tablespoon hot water

Preheat oven to 350°. Grease a 9-inch square pan. In a large bowl, combine flour, ginger, and cinnamon. In a smaller bowl, combine melted butter, molasses, and 1 cup hot water. Add molasses mixture to flour mixture and stir until combined. Stir in baking soda mixture. Bake for 30 to 40 minutes or until a toothpick inserted in the center comes out clean.

Serve with ice cream, another of Dolley's favorites.

FURTHER READING

NONFICTION
Carter, Alden R. *The War of 1812: Second Fight for Independence.* Danbury, CT: Franklin Watts, 1993. An introduction to the War of 1812.

Waters, Kate. *The Story of the White House.* New York: Scholastic, 1992. A photo-illustrated history of the White House.

FICTION
Greeson, Janet. *An American Army of Two.* Minneapolis: Carolrhoda, 1992. An adventure based on the true story of two young women who turned the tables on the powerful British army during the War of 1812.

Robinet, Harriet Gillem. *Washington City Is Burning.* New York: Simon & Schuster, 1996. The story of a young slave girl working for the Madisons who experiences the burning of Washington.

WEBSITES

The Dolley Madison Project
<moderntimes.vcdh.virginia.edu/madison> Detailed history of Dolley Madison's life, including timelines, photographs, and letters.

Montpelier
<www.montpelier.org> Contains biographical information about James and Dolley Madison, as well as information about Montpelier, their Virginia home.

SELECT BIBLIOGRAPHY

Arnett, Ethel Stephens. *Mrs. James Madison: The Incomparable Dolley.* Greensboro, NC: Piedmont Press, 1972.

Correspondence of Dolley Payne Madison, from the files of The Papers of James Madison. University of Virginia, Charlottesville, VA.

The Cutts Collection. Library of Congress, Washington, DC.

Dolley Madison Papers. Special Collections. University of Virginia Library, Charlottesville, VA.

Gould, Lewis L., ed. *American First Ladies: Their Lives and Legacy.* New York: Garland Publishing, 1996.

Hunt-Jones, Conover. *Dolley and the "great little Madison."* Washington, DC: American Institute of Architects Press, 1977.

Ketcham, Ralph. *James Madison: A Biography.* Charlottesville, VA: The University Press of Virginia, 1990.

Mattern, David, and Holly C. Shulman. *The Selected Letters of Dolley Payne Madison.* Charlottesville, VA: The University Press of Virginia, forthcoming.

The Papers of Dolley Madison. Library of Congress, Washington, DC.

Pitch, Anthony S. *The Burning of Washington: The British Invasion of 1814.* Annapolis, MD: Naval Institute Press, 1998.

Smith, Margaret Bayard. Ed. Gaillard Hunt. *The First Forty Years of Washington Society.* New York: Charles Scribners Sons, 1906.

INDEX

Acknowledgments

For photographs and artwork: © North Wind Picture Archives, pp. 4, 7, 11, 20, 27, 28, 33, 39; © Bettmann/CORBIS, p. 8; © Lee Snider/CORBIS, p. 10; © Virginia Historical Society, pp. 12, 15, 32; © Hulton Getty/Getty Images, pp. 17, 42; © Greensboro Historical Museum, pp. 18, 23, 41; © Stock Montage, pp. 19, 24, 26, 35, 36; The White House Collection, courtesy the White House Historical Association, p. 25. Front cover courtesy of Stock Montage. Back cover courtesy of Corbis Royalty Free Images.

For quoted material: p. 11, Lucia Beverley Cutts, *Memoirs and Letters of Dolly Madison, Wife of James Madison, President of the United States* (Boston: Houghton Mifflin, 1886); pp. 20, 36, The Cutts Collection, Library of Congress, Washington, DC; p. 21, American State Papers, 1814; p. 24, Paul Jennings, *A Colored Man's Reminiscences of James Madison* (Brooklyn, 1865); pp. 25, 40, The Papers of Dolley Madison, Library of Congress, Washington, DC; p. 30, Jennings, *Reminiscences;* p. 32, Margaret Bayard Smith, *The First Forty Years of Washington Society* (New York: Charles Scribners Sons, 1906); p. 43, Edith P. Mayo, ed., *The Smithsonian Book of First Ladies* (New York: Henry Holt, 1996).